DOROTHY BETTENCOURT ELFSTROM

Challenge

of the

Seasons

by
DOROTHY BETTENCOURT ELFSTROM

The Naylor Company
Book Publishers of the Southwest
San Antonio, Texas

To My Children

> With the hope that these words may
> be of some inspiration to guide
> them in their journey through the
> seasons.

Preface

A lifetime is but a day in the sight of God. I would say that the moment of his understanding of this fact gives birth to the most pleasing and satisfying era of man's tenure of life on earth — to his Creator and to himself, for then he knows why he is here and what he has to do.

A few experience this moment in the Spring, but to many it does not occur until Fall or Winter.

Each season poses special challenges of all of us, and we find that life is like an absorbing novel — we can't wait to see what will happen on the next page, yet knowing all the while that each chapter brings us nearer to the end.

In the poems that follow — written through the years — I have tried to capture some of the joys and the sorrows, the dreams, hopes and philosophies that one might encounter in meeting the challenge of the seasons.

Acknowledgments and Thanks

Grateful acknowledgment is given to the following publications in which certain of these poems have appeared: *Saturday Evening Post, Good Housekeeping, Radio Mirror, True Confessions,* Ted Malone's *Between the Bookends, Christian Home, The Market Research Scholarship Fund Newsletter, Secrets,* The Galveston Daily *News,* The Galveston *Tribune, Judge, Ideals, Food for Thought, Romance, Ten Story Love, Galveston Isle, Chipmunk, Living Quill, Beat of Wings, All-Story Love, Love Short Stories, Sanctuary, The Think Tank, Happiness, Embers,* The Texas City *Sun,* Dee Walker's *The Poet's Corner, Candor, The House of Moody, The Covered Wagon, Hearth Songs, Sage, Liberty, Physical Culture, The American Courier, The Improvement Era, Wildfire,* Warp's *Christmas Messenger.*

My gratitude to the following radio readers for using some of these poems on the air: Ted Malone, Don McNeill, Dee Walker, Meador Lowrey and Bill Webb.

To Esther Baldwin York and Toni Noel, for their esteemed poetic counsel. Special thanks to my Heavenly Father for entrusting me with the talent for writing; to Margaret Catherine and Henry Joseph Bettencourt for fostering that talent by being such inspirational parents and eager listeners, to my deceased husband, Walter William Elfstrom; our children, Dorothy, Bill and Henry; and all other relatives and friends for their encouragement and enthusiasm along the way.

List of Illustrations

Contents

Spring

Spring

Fit or Misfit

New lovers and new pairs of shoes
Should be acquired with special care;
They both come pretty as you choose,
But some were never made for wear.

Yoicks!

Each man is born a hound at heart,
For hunting is a manly art;
His instincts clamor to pursue
And tree his harassed love anew
Each day.
    To make a romance last,
Girls, run the course — but not too fast!

"A dream in the heart is worth more than a fortune in each hand."

Dreams

Dreams are bright, elusive things
With rainbow gowns. On golden wings
They drift along just out of reach;
Although our hearts beg and beseech
Their favors, they elude the touch
Of human hands, slip through our clutch,
Inviting further, vain pursuit
Their freedom won beyond dispute.

"Hem-haw"

While the girls were making beelines
For the mid-calf "hide-your-knee" lines,
Guys were favoring the hemlines
That divulged much more of stemlines —
Thus: the famous last "Ah, men!" lines.

The Charmer

April, the charmer in daffodil dress
With strawberry lips that invite a caress,
Has a heart that's as light as the cool mountain breeze,
And she has brought many a man to his knees.

She's the darling of springtime, from what some will say,
While others prefer her demure sister, May,
But April is wild and her smile is bewitching,
And a guard on the heart will save plenty of stitching.

So take what she whispers with two grains of salt,
For a changeable mood is her only bad fault;
She is fun to be with for she's full of surprise —
But take care you don't drown in her rain-spangled eyes.

When Mother Earth Awakens

When Mother Earth dons her new bonnet
Of yellow and white daffodils
And her dress with the violet tip on it
To match slippers of violet spills;

When butterflies fashion her shoulder
A fanciful, fluttering stole,
And mankind's heart grows a bit bolder
To conquer his love and his goal;

When Mother Earth lovingly cradles
The newborn in meadow and tree,
Excited spring lavishly ladles
Inspiration to dreamers like me.

Leap, Dear

From his tactless remarks I am truly afraid
What he's looking for isn't a wife but a maid.
With leap year supplying no conquests to plume,
I shall marry him — then we'll see who waits on whom.

Mischievous March Wind

The wind is a mischievous boy today
Going home from school, in the mood for play;
He lifts the tresses of ruffled girls
And lets them fall in tangled swirls.

He takes a hat from a cocky head
And carries it off to a muddy bed;
He roars at the plants beginning to flower
And frightens them till they cringe and cower.

But then — after all day's gadding about,
Twilight comes, and he's tuckered out,
And Mother Earth, understandingly,
Lulls him into tranquility.

Off the Hit Parade

Yesterday you broke my heart —
Strange how much it mattered —
Letters that you didn't write,
Love you wildly scattered.

But someone came along today
Who does a neater rhumba,
Which renders you, my "tried untrue,"
A less disturbing number.

Restless

Like a sea gull I ever am restless
As I travel the Great Voyage of Life;
Daydreams are the wings that transport me
Away from the cares and the strife

Of the routinous things that grow boresome;
My soul craves adventure — romance;
I thrill to the notes of great music;
My feet long to march and to dance.

Sometimes when the world bears down on me
Like a cage with iron bars,
I gaze at the blue sky above me,
Finding freedom among the stars,

Or in the sweet song of the robin,
Or the waves of the onrushing sea;
Somehow I feel kin to the ocean,
For it, too, seems restless like me.

My heart seeks out warmth — understanding,
My mind, greater knowledge of things,
And I'm thankful that I was born restless
With the thundering urge of wings.

So Sorry

You tell me that your other loves
Were just to raise my dander,
But, as they say, what's sauce for goose
Is *haute cuisine* for gander.

Now that your love is all for me,
Somehow I'm as you used to be.

Earth-Bound

Once I looked upon you
    As my guiding star;
Always I was wretched,
    Wishing from afar.
Thank you, dear, for proving
    How earth-bound you are.

Tips—"Tops"

He who grows averse to tipping
Soon finds his importance slipping.

Human Nature

Why is it we like strawberries best
When they are out of season?
Or long for the adventures that
We know are out of reason?

And why do we enjoy the most
The sports where there is danger?
What makes us fascinated by
A devilish-looking stranger?

Why is it that when summer's here
Our preference is cold weather?
Why do we hate to be apart
Yet quarrel when we're together?

Perhaps it's human nature to
Desire the unattainable,
And things are less attractive when
We find that they are gainable.

To a Restaurant Bun

Brown, brick-batty little bun,
Since others left you quite unharmed,
Answer to this ravenous one —
How many times have you been warmed?

Difference of Opinion

You say you'd like to take me out
And buy me steak for dinner;
Then to the movie we would go —
You tell me you're no sinner —

That by the time the clock struck ten
You'd have me home to Mother,
No out of gas or tire gone flat —
You'd treat me as a brother.

I told my mom, and she said, "No"
Because she won't believe me;
And I'd appeal the case if I
Imagined you'd deceive me.

Unpredictable

Don't sigh because you've been betrayed
By April, who's a fickle maid.
Pick up your heart and start anew. . . .
This April's not the girl for you,
For she's an adolescent child
Whose dreams are very young and wild,
And in the springtide of her life
She wouldn't make a faithful wife.
Give her more time to grow and play,
Perhaps she'll settle down some day.

11

But—Thinking It Over

He would be bad for you, my dear;
There's too much wolf blood in him,
And his inconstancy, I hear,
Would make it hard to win him.
Is that he standing at the gate?
Quick! Take a look! Are my seams straight?

On Second Thought

You speak to me of love that's free
    Of rules and regulations,
No wedding ring nor anything
    To cause us complications.

You say if I can love that way
    You'll humor all my wishes,
And that I'll never weep nor sweep,
    Nor have to do the dishes.

You tempt me, sir, I can't deny it,
But not enough for me to try it.

Just Wondering

When I'm with you I always find
I simply can't make up my mind
If I would have you think I'm, say,
The kind of girl of Grandma's day,
Or that I'm just a modern miss
Who doesn't mind a goodnight kiss.
The question is — oh lucky sir,
Which type of girl do you prefer?

Exclusive

You play the field and have your fun —
You're free and over twenty-one,
So there's no reason why you shouldn't
And none for me to wish you wouldn't.
But don't expect to mix my kisses
With those of all the other misses.

Not Too Nice

Some say all little girls are nice
Because they're made of sugar 'n spice,
But most of what composes me
I dare say must be T. N. T.
What else could cause such wild delight
Whenever you come into sight —
Unless it could be dynamite?

Provocative

I'm jealous of you and your glamorous past,
Notwithstanding that I should know better;
Although his lips touched you and he held you last,
I'm foolish — you're only a letter.

Wishing

If I were an elf tonight
I'd perch upon that crescent moon,
Grab a star in each hand and
Bang them together like cymbals,
Hoping that star chips would fall upon your pillow
And that you would dream about the one who loves you.

Adventurer

What am I seeking,
Haunting the sky —
Gathering stardust —
Where do I fly?
Is there a place where
I'd be content,
Or will I drift till
My life has been spent?
I'll not complain if
This IS Fate's decree —
Soaring is very
Exciting to me!

I Hope—I Hope Not

You wouldn't like her type, I'm sure,
She's scatterbrained and immature.
Her voice is loud — her manners bad,
Her giggle nearly drives one mad.

Of course, she thinks she's worldy-wise
With that come-hither in her eyes.
And she's the type who'd try to woo you;
You wouldn't think she's cute — or DO you?

15

Different Ways

Yours is the kind of kiss I can't afford.
Yours are the sort of dreams I will not share.
You should have been a dashing knight with sword —
To risk my heart with you I wouldn't dare.

You have an innate longing for the moon.
My wish — a house with daisies, row on row.
You'd be content at first, but all too soon
Freedom would beckon and you'd long to go.

Let's say goodbye while there is great esteem
In both our hearts — no bitterness nor doubt,
Going our separate ways, each to his dream —
You who can't live within walls, I, without.

I Wonder

I think I love you. I'm not sure
How much, or that it will endure;
I only know that when you're near
My heart soars into stratosphere.
Are you the one Fate meant for me?
Please kiss me, sweet, so I may see.

"Ha—Sweet Mystery"

You look at me,
And I can see
You wonder what I'm thinking;
I gaze at you
And wonder too
Just what's behind that winking.

You plainly show
You'd like to know
If I find you appealing;
Yet you disguise
With laughing eyes
Your every thought and feeling.

And thus we chat
Of this and that,
Not hinting we're debating,
And aim to guess,
Come now — confess —
Just what is meditating.

On Some Future Day

When you remember me,
The vision of the face you held between
    your hands may have grown dim,
The hair you smoothed from troubled
    brow,
The lips you kissed with sudden, mad
    desire,
The eyelashes that were wet with tears
    when you departed —
All may have become blurred in your
    memory,
But you won't forget that our souls met,
And that is all important . . . .

Ups and Downs

Along life's rugged highways
We have our up-and-down days —
Some days we seem to soar so high
We bump our heads against the sky;
While other days we sail so low
Beneath a bridge we couldn't go —
But why it is I do not know.

Me vs. Me

The bad little me says I love him
And hungrily crave his caress;
The good little me is embarrassed
And very bewildered, I guess.

The nice little me does her darndest
Most always to try to disguise
Her feelings — the naughty me wants to
Wear come-hither looks in her eyes.

The saintly me passes up chances
The sinner me gladly would take;
Conventional me beams approval,
While primitive me chides, "You fake!"

Which makes life, perhaps, most exciting:
The two me's are ever in bout,
While I chew my nails at the ringside
And wonder who's knocking whom out.

Heart, Be Steady!

Heart, be steady — do not quicken
When they mention April's name.
She's as changeable as ever,
So, I ask — have you no shame?

Surely you must well remember
Last spring's enervating chase.
Yes, I'll grant it was exciting,
But we finished second place!

Don't be charmed by the daffodils
April's wearing in her hair.
They're just more of her designing.
Heart, be still — or do we dare?

Beggar

A beggar at the table of her love,
He stands by, waiting for the crumbs that fall,
Or that she tosses out so recklessly;
She does not heed the longing, tender call —

Of his heart to her own — The pain of love
That's unreturned she, too, finds hard to bear,
Ears deafened by the pounding of her heart
For someone else who is not standing there.

Reflections

Some day when we are old and hours weigh
Upon our hands like tears upon the heart,
And you have time, I rather think you may
Regret the deeds that cause us now to part.

While youth is pulsing hotly through the veins
And every moment's filled, we are inclined
To frown on serious thought as growing pains,
Preferring lighter musing for the mind.

Some day when we are old, perhaps you'll write
And tell me that you spent a lonely night.

Apology

I said goodbye today to every dream
We ever shared and all the plans we made;
To your cool reasoning it wouldn't seem
That now I could be sorry and afraid.
How easily the angry lips impart
Words that have no endorsement of the heart.

Always It's You

Always, beyond the rim of time or space
There is your face
Haunting my reverie.
How comforting your sweet, enchanting smile
That shortens waiting hours and many a mile
For me.

Language of Love

I thought that I could lend my heart
    For just a while
To the enchantment of your touch —
    Your slow, sweet smile.

But when I sought to take it back,
    To my surprise
I found that you could hold it fast
    With just your eyes.

Summer

Sacred Hour

A quaint old chapel on the hill
    With chapel bells that broke the still,
Two hearts that beat in perfect time,
    Resounding echo of a chime.
A question, and the answer, "Yes";
    A gentle voice that said, "God bless
You children —" just as day was done:
    Two souls uniting into one.

Moment, Stand Still

Moment, stand still — there can be no returning;
Soon you'll be only a part of the past.
This is the hour for which I have been yearning,
But like a snowflake, though held, you won't last.

Cradled by love is this night of fulfillment,
Only you know of the joy you have brought.
From over the rainbow you came with instillment
Of flame in the heart which I so long have sought.

Moment, stand still in your raiment of rapture;
Dance in the moonlight and hold back the dawn.
Your magic spell I can never recapture,
And only in memory will you live on.

Season's Bride

June is the heart of summer,
Tender and warm and true,
Flush with springtime's farewell kiss,
Ardently eager to woo.

She is the bride of the seasons,
Daisies adorn her brow;
Her sweetness and charms are reasons
For love's most sacred vow.

June is a favorite with children,
Who all adore her ways,
Well knowing that she comes bringing
Sunny vacation days.

No Vacancy

Her heart was a furnished apartment
That she rented now and then,
Her tenants a changing assortment —
She wasn't impressed with men.

He came. From the sound of her laughter,
I knew that renting would cease,
And it wasn't long thereafter
That she gave him a life-time lease.

Bride Fixing Dinner

Tell me, what would you like to eat —
Beans or beets or spinach, my sweet?
Black-eyed peas or corned beef hash,
Candied yams or succotash?
Why leave it to me — please state your "druther" —
One defrosts as quick as another.

Not So Dumb

"Study, Rose, as Molly does —"
The family did beseech 'er
Till Molly won the scholarship
And Rosie won the teacher.

Better Never Late

Nancy took her time to dress;
Never was she ready
When her young man came to call
(He was then her steady).
There was Sue, her little sis,
Who dressed in just a minute.
When the wedding did take place
Nancy wasn't in it.

To A Bridegroom

There will be other girls, of that I'm sure,
Whose beauty will inspire a backward glance;
There may come one who even will endure
For long enough to put you in a trance.
But be assured, my dear, I do not think
That she will be the one who gets the mink.

Galveston at Oleander Time

Like welcoming arms, their branches are outspread,
Adorned with blossoms from the deepest red
To purest white and blends of softer hue,
Each adding its enchantment to the view.
Refreshed by last night's rain, they face the sun —
It's oleander time in Galveston!

On The Beach

TO A SEA GULL

Where are you bound,
Oh, pilferer of the ocean's stores?
Lend me your wings to venture
Up through heaven's doors.

TO A SEA SHELL

You are a lovely piece of art
With your beauty there unfurled,
Glistening in the moonlight
From a sandy world.

TO A BIT OF SEA FOAM

Fluffy bit of sea foam,
Scurrying about,
I watch you smaller, smaller grow
Till the wind has blown you out.

July

July is a tall glass of pink lemonade,
Firecrackers, flags and the gay Fourth parade.
It's big beach umbrellas and plenty of shade.
July is vacations and oodles of fun,
And getting a tan in the sizzling sun.
It's sailboats, romance and another heart won.
July is swim suits bobbing out of the blue;
It's dancing and dreaming and fanciful view.
It's my favorite month, for July gave me you.

The Last Word

A feather in your cap, you say
You've won our little spat;
I'll wear a feather, too, that's gay
In a forty-dollar hat!

To A Witch

You, witch who share my husband's working day,
If you but knew, I envy you each one —
The banter you exchange — the irking way
He leans upon you, and when day is done
Comes home and tells about your new hair style,
Oh, so becoming! Or your chic black dress,
And I must beam agreeably the while
I'm tempted . . . how I'd like to . . . well . . . you guess!

But after dinner, when the lights are low,
And I am in his arms with love's swift fires,
Your charms are soon forgotten, that I know,
And once again I'm all that he requires.
Then always I suspect he used your name
To fan my love into a brighter flame.

A Woman Waits

Woman spends much of her life
Waiting for her man to return
From work, from the sea, or from battle,
From hunting or fishing,
From preoccupied mind . . . .
To the warmth of her love —
The greatness of her understanding —
Because he needs her
In order to feel complete.
And she is never truly content
Until he is there beside her.

Question Before The House

A most perplexing problem
To husbands, so they say,
Is trying to imagine
What housewives do all day.

To An Unenlightened Benedict

Like a spirited colt you're straining at the reins,
Expecting me to draw them in —
Your reasoning's thin.
How well I know that, if I hope to win,
I must sustain the feckless heart that feigns
Indifference and give you slack,
So that one day, you'll turn, amazed to find
That I am idling far behind.
I hope my seeming not to mind
Will bring you racing back.

Tell Me

Why, preceding wedding bells
Do we get a honeyed look that spells,
"Talk to me, you cute creation,
Give out with the conversation"?
While after, it's a lemon-baited
Glance implying "Okeh, state it
If you must, but make it snappy,
Then let me read, and I'll be happy."

"Bridle, Sweet"

Experienced at ropin',
She can well afford to brag
That she changed him from unbroken
Colt into a steady nag.

Chef Salad

I may not bake the lightest cake
Nor serve the most delicious steak;
Nor can I sew the neatest seam –
But I can weave a lovely dream,
And life without its dreams, to me,
Is summer lunch without iced tea.

The "Man" in Him

After I slaved the whole week through
In spite of fever 102,
And Sunday, with a splitting head,
Reluctantly I took to bed,
My lord, without intent to vex,
Begged pardon for "the weaker sex."

Uh Huh

You are indeed the perfect spouse,
As unobtrusive as a mouse;
You do not waste the merest glance
On other women when we dance;
You'd never flirt by grin or wink —
At least, that's what you think I think.

Husband's Blessing

Bless all frozen pastry bakers,
Even more bless all wig makers!
Horrid pin-ups so unsightly
(Gouging metal armor nightly)
Are covered now by glamour tresses
Much more suited to caresses.

Introduction, Please!

Be there a man, alive or dead,
Who to some damsel hasn't said,
"We will forever dance and dine
If you, fair beauty, will be mine?"
(Be there a man, alive or dead,
Who later fulfilled what he said?)

Off-Spring

Wishing

Oh, to be a child again,
And fancy the dreams that a child dreams!
Wasn't it only yesterday when
Life was a round of enchanting schemes?

What could come up to the make-believe
Of the games we played and the books we read,
And the fantasies we would always weave
When the lights were dimmed and our prayers said?

Oh, to recapture a child's faith,
With the sweet contentment that it brings;
Kings would exchange their empires for
A child's delight in the simple things!

First-born

I can't yet realize that she is ours —
This precious little bundle — heaven-sent.
Those big blue eyes — that tiny, winsome smile —
I'm glad it was for our house she was meant!

God could have mailed her elsewhere, and we'd not
Have known the joy in just her baby grip
Upon our fingers, nor the trusting way
She looks at us that makes our heartbeats skip.

So new to us — she still seems like a dream —
Too perfect and too marvelous to be.
Another day dawns — joyfully we find
That she's still here and belongs to you and me.

Chip off The Old Block

Our daughter asked me for the moon tonight,
And there was eager pleading in her eyes.
Her chubby hands were raised in wild delight;
I knew she would accept no compromise.

Her dolly? No! That wouldn't do at all —
She put it from her with impatient thrust;
I didn't have the heart (she is so small)
To tell her compromises are a must.

I bribed her with a Christmas bauble, glad
To find one for her curious eyes to see.
The day she learns the moon cannot be had
I wonder if she'll try convincing me.

Ho Hum----

Get thee behind me, cozy bed,
  And do not further tempt me;
You know that Junior must be fed —
  "Hush, boy! Are you *THAT* empty?"

Confirmation

I had no way of knowing what you thought —
Or what you were expecting, dear, to see,
But Junior brought the answer that I sought: —
"Why, honey, he's a replica of me!"

Note to All Fathers of Sons

They are *your* boys, and whatever they do
Is going to be patterned after you —
The rules you live by, your words, your goals
Will remain with them as smouldering coals,
For Dad is their hero, and in their eyes
There is none more perfect and none more wise.

They want to be like you in every way,
And they'll be observing you day by day
To learn how you cope with the problems of life
And how you react to the struggle and strife —
How you distinguish the good from the bad;
You're the living example to your small lad.

When the day has been rugged and feelings show through,
Its trials will soon be forgotten by you,
But you can't erase the impatience you dare
Toward those whom God lent you for guidance and care;
For it's not just on Sundays and holidays
That they follow your footsteps and watch your ways.

Encouragement

A pat on the head from a fellow's dad,
Or his mother's approving smile
Lets him know right off that his world is glad
And secure for another while.

Gifts may impress, but the glow will die
That's attached to a fine new toy,
But the gift of love that coins can't buy
Will live in the heart of a boy.

If You Know There Are Folks

If you know there are folks who are counting on you,
Who care if you don't make the grade, or you do,
Who are proud of your every good thought and good deed,
You will work a lot harder to try to succeed.

And when obstacles loom up and get in your way
And you might be inclined to give up, you will stay
In and pitch, even though you be heartsick and blue —
For you can't let those down who are counting on you.

Paternity

Enjoy them for the brief time they are yours —
All too soon they will want to try their wings;
While respites are welcome, quiet that endures
Is bound to have its lonely, saddening stings.

The love they give is pure; the simple trust
They place in you is heavenly to hold,
So guard it well, or it may turn to dust;
And know its worth — more valuable than gold.

When rampant energies goad you to display
Antagonism, try to understand,
Remembering all too soon will come the day
When someone else will hold that little hand.

Problems of A School Boy

My pop thinks a boy should be
Perfect to the nth degree —
Scrubbed and on the dot for dinner,
Lessons up — a gold-star winner,
Garbage emptied, lawn in trim
(There is no sweet-talking him)
After which is time for fun,
But, gee whiz, Pop, *then* day is done!

To A Devoted Master

A lonely, scared, bewildered kitten
Out in the cold without his fittin' —
Whom to take up with? Whither to roam?
For who would be caring I had no home?
Turned out to learn to live by my wits
In a world full of dogs who would tear me to bits.

Then *you* with a heart as big as my sigh
One day just chanced to be passing by.
You seemed to sense my muted fear
For you wiped away an unshed tear.
You held me close, and then I knew
From that day forth I'd belong to you.

Oh, Kindly Hand, oh, happy day
That guided your path to the little stray.
    — "Tiger."

First Orchid

Shyly he handed the box to her,
Watching her questioning eyes,
That were becoming a misty blur
As she opened her "big surprise."

"An orchid! My! What a lovely sight!
It's the first that I ever had!"
As if her heart would burst with delight
She hugged the blue-eyed lad.

"It's a little droopy, Miss Eaves," he said,
"Someone lost it, I guess."
The teacher patted his curly head
And pinned the flower to her dress.

Observations of An Eight-year Old

It didn't take me long to learn
That though Dad's big, brown hands can earn
More money and can chop more wood
Than Mom's small white ones ever could,
And for some reason make you feel
Safer when they're at the wheel,

If dreams that make him shake with fright
Awaken a fellow in the night
While Mom's out, buying a baby sister,
Or if his shoe has rubbed a blister,
Or a button pops and must have sewing,
And the gang is anxious to get going,
Dad's hands get all stiff and numb,
As if each finger were a thumb.

June

June means a boy with his cane fishing pole;
Since school is dismissed he has no other goal
Than daydreaming, scheming, and just having fun.
Already his face has been kissed by the sun
Till tiny brown freckles are out everywhere.
But he isn't bothered — his slim feet are bare,
And he wiggles his toes, making plan after plan
For the day when his years will proclaim him a man.

*M*adly crammin' facts and figures

*I*nto heads that throb and pound —

*D*arn the TV that is blastin'!

*T*elephone? I can't be found!

*E*at? Oh, what a mad suggestion!

*R*ate I'm goin' it will be

*M*ornin' and I'll still be at it —

*E*ver faithful, studious me.

X-ray brain is what I'm needin',

*A*spirin surely I could use —

*M*om, toss me a pillow, will you?

*S*pare me fifteen for a snooze.

September Setting

The kids look sizes bigger;
The desks seem rather small
To bridle so much energy —
Eyes wander to the hall.

The teacher calls for order,
But the word has lost its force,
For in June, July, and August
Freedom ran her course.

Can't hear above the hubbub,
And everything seems strange,
But past experience tells me
Tomorrow things will change.

Grand Finale

She watched his animated face
    In keen anticipation.
He said the words that filled her heart
    With pride and much elation.
He took her tiny hand in his;
    June lent her spiced aroma
As once again the president
    Presented a diploma.

Religion

It's not just saying "Hi" to God on Sunday mornings bright,
Nor murmuring a prayer or two before we sleep at night;
It's knowing our Creator's near each moment night and day
And showing Him we know He is by doing things His way.

It can't be gained by good deeds done with boasting or
    complaints;
It won't rub off upon us even if we sit with saints;
It can't be bought with coins nor with gems piled mountain-
    high;
It can't be given to us if we've not the faith to try.

It's not just loving those we like but family, friend, and foe
And filling life so full of love that greed and envy go;
It's living life as Jesus taught — the humble, thoughtful way
And doing all the good we can each hour of every day.

Gramp, The Novice

Bring your thread, Mom, and your big
    needle, please,
For I have a date with a honey;
They tell me she's blonde and the right
    size to squeeze,
With a smile that is dimpled and sunny.
Our Johnny just called — says the blonde
    looks like me —
Imagine it, Mom! Like the Suttons!
Hospital visiting hour is at three,
And the old man just busted his buttons!

Lines to A Son

If the crowd takes a path that you think may be wrong
And implies that you must or you just don't belong,
Let them know without shame that you won't go along,
For it takes a real man to be different.

It won't require brains to fall in like a sheep,
And it doesn't take skill to get lost in the deep,
For even an ash can be part of the heap,
But it takes a real man to be different.

Fall-in-liners are many, like corn on the cob,
For no courage or thought is required in a gob.
Anyone who conforms can be part of the mob,
But it takes a real man to be different.

Note to A Son:

I hope you know that love comes from the heart;
For though the hair may be like pure spun gold
And though the form may give delight to hold,
These count for naught when two must face life's test;
My son, you know I want for you what's best.
Remember well, and when you choose be wise —
Let beauty not be blinding to your eyes;
For beauty that you see is but a shell.
The beauty that's within is what will tell.

Autumn

The Gypsy Girl

October is a gypsy girl
With skirt of autumn leaves that whirl
As she dances barefoot down the night —
Indeed a most bewitching sight!
　　Her stole of yellow mums she flings
　　Into the pumpkin patch and sings
　　A love song to Ole Mister Moon,
　　Who winks and wishes he could croon.
Amid the late-husked corn she skips,
The stain of grape jam on her lips,
Brushing away the cobweb lace
That seeks to veil her pretty face.
　　She laughs at Ole Man Winter's threat
　　That dancers pay "the Piper's debt,"
　　Till Jack Frost catches the harvest belle
　　And nips her toes to break the spell.

Dwarfed

Duties
Are the guards
That hold prisoners
Our thoughts,

And he who takes
No time out for dreaming
Not only stoops his shoulders
But also his soul.

Halloween Time

October is a harvest moon
With romance in his genial beam —
Hayrides to a football tune —
The essence of a student's dream.

October is an orange field
Of pumpkins ripe upon the vine,
And jars of air Jack Frost unsealed
That are as tipsying as wine.

October is a frosty sky
Where witches roam and snowflakes brew.
Say, there's a witch with evil eye!
And hear the owl keep asking "Who — o — oo?"

The Eleventh Month

Take a day that is blessed with warm sunshine;
Add a leaf just turned gold and one brown.
Open bottles of air, crisp — with essence of pine,
Find football in any home town.
Gather dreams and a fireplace — remember?
Grab a turkey that's well-fed and spry;
Combine for delightful November,
And, of course, don't forget the mince pie!

Give Us This Day

We thank You, Lord, for giving us this day —

Last night as the storm raged and it seemed that for us there might not be a tomorrow we were full of fear and regret —

Fear that on this day we might be facing You and having to give an account of our stewardship,

And regret that we hadn't said and done all that we might have, to be worthy of Your love — to feel confident that You would ask us to enter into Your kingdom.

But then — as suddenly as it had come — the storm subsided and we knew that You had given us a second chance.

May we never forget the fear of those dreadful moments and the resolutions that we made.

And when we are praying, "Give us this day —,"
Let us ever add, "To live each moment of it according to
                                Your will,"

And again we say, from the bottom of our hearts,
We thank You, Lord, for giving us this day.

Rebellious Cherub

Don't strain your eyes, dear, I exhort,
For if I wore my shorts that short
Would I meet with enthusiasm?
Not yet, while you possess sarcasm.
If my costumes were that revealing,
Your modesty would hit its ceiling.

Enjoy the role of saint I won't
While you enjoy the girls who don't.

The Indiscreet Chrysanthemums

Defiant of November's sober skies,
They flaunt their colors in the frosty air.
With gaiety and mischief in their eyes
They scoff at Old Man Winter's icy stare.

He's standing in the wing of Nature's stage,
Impatient to begin his ruthless role;
Accompanied by winds that moan and rage,
He muses of his wicked, nearing goal.

"Those flowers shall lose their heads,"
        they hear him growl,
And though they realize their timely fate
And hear the north wind's angry, answering howl,
Today they live — tomorrow is too late!

Tell Me—Must You?

Must you ogle every damsel
As she's promenading by?
Won't we ever pass a girl
Who fails to magnetize your eye?

Must you learn if each has ankles
And their size and shape and such?
If a bit of knee is showing,
Do you have to know how much?

Must you then size up her lines
As you would a horse to race?
Must your eyes engage her eyes
As you are meeting face to face?

Must you compliment her highly
In your silent, subtle way?
If you must, you might remember
I expect the same bouquet.

Housewife's Prayer

Dear Lord, please help me on this day
To find a more efficient way
To cook his meals and make the beds,
To bathe the kids and scrub their heads,
To wash and iron, to scour and sew —
(This is a big request, I know)
And if it's too much, as I fear,
Inform my man — it's his idea.

Impenetrable

You haven't said your heart's no longer mine,
Yet there's a hint in everything you do.
Your kiss that used to be a lover's sign
Is flat; your conversation's different too,

As if you measure every phrase you say
With words intended for a stranger's ear.
You stare, and yet your thoughts are far away,
And often when I speak, you do not hear.

Somehow I wish we'd face the bitter facts —
The sword is so much quicker than the ax.

The Bible

Fountain of wisdom, eternally true,
When I am troubled I turn to you.
Drinking your words that refresh my tired soul,
Seeking the light to make clearer my goal,
Finding new courage and strength to proceed —
Ever the spiritual food that I need.

The "Other" Woman

I used to pray to love you more and more,
Not knowing too much loving isn't good
For restless men; it sometimes tends to bore
And turn the glance — not saying that it would.
Now, being older — wiser, too, I guess,
I pray that I will learn to love you less.

Passing Fancy

She's gorgeous — that I will have to admit,
With her taffy hair — I don't blame you a bit
For taking another look or two —
Or has your gaze wavered since she's been in view?

Her frock is neat and up to the minute,
And you are so right — she does fit well in it.
No ring third finger? She's fancy free!
But unfortunately, dear, you belong to me.

Love's Reward

In each romance there's one who loves the most,
With more ideals and gentler, kindlier touch;
Of victory banners he has few to boast,
Who loves more deeply, possibly too much.

He is the first to try to gain a truce
After the heat of argument has cooled;
Always for his beloved he'll make excuse;
He is the one most likely to be fooled.

But love is its own reward and recompenses
For all of the little hurts and slight offenses.

Meditations of An Old Flame

You rave to me of all her charms,
This dream Fate led into your arms.
At every chance you speak her name,
Yet in your much-too-loud acclaim
I'm wondering — which would it be?
Are you convincing you or me?

"Hell Hath No Fury...."

The girls who came before I do not mind,
But heaven help the girl who comes behind.

Go Quickly

Let us remember only love's swift spring,
When every kiss inspired a rhapsody;
Dwell not upon the bitter nor the sting —
Then if you should some day return to me
There will be no expressions to rescind
Before our hearts may dance upon the wind.

"Yes, Squire"

Here is the face to charm a million men.
Notice those eyes of dangerous beckoning.
Hers is the likeness fashioned for your den,
And with that heart there is no reckoning.

Hers is the smile to haunt your waking hours,
Yet she's one lass I'll never have to doubt,
For with her beauty fresh as April showers,
Thank heaven she's well-bound and can't get out.

The Glass Turned Down

Today I severed every legal tie
And gave you back the freedom that you sought;
Now you may meet adventure eye to eye
Without a pause for conscientious thought.
You will not travel far before you find
That ties which hold the heart do not unwind.

Without You

How can I face tomorrow without you,
Who gave a meaning to my every thought?
Closing love's door to start my life anew,
Turning from all the happiness you brought?

How can I make my sad heart understand
You won't be back to share the passing days?
That not again will we walk hand in hand —
How can a heart in love change all its ways?

How can a soul who found serenity
In just your presence, learn to grope alone?
Vision your face with no identity?
Think of your name and not call you my own?

How can I face tomorrow — it would seem
This should turn out to all be but a dream.

Goodbye

Bask in your new-won freedom;
Roam to your heart's content;
Say that our days together
Turned into years ill spent.

Boast of your landlady's cooking;
Swear it will make you fat,
But get off my doorstep, will you? —
It's time to put out the cat.

Community Property

To my surprise this morning
I found myself bereft
Not only of my husband
But my toothbrush since he left.

Day of Reckoning

If you, my love, return to me
I'll welcome you with open arms.
The honey on my tongue will be
As sweet as my remembered charms.
And when you're sure I'll have you back
I'll smile — and send you off to pack.

Terminal

Tread lightly through my thoughts. Do not delay
For long enough to stoke the dying fire.
My heart is weak — do not induce its sway
With mad desire.

I must forget there ever was a you,
Who brought to me an unrelenting glow
And keep before me what I have to do —
Please go.

Reunion

For weeks I had pictured our meeting.
After three long years, it would be dramatic —
A little embarrassing.
We would be shy — strangers almost,
And before the crowd of people at the station
You would embrace me lightly,
And your eyes would take in my face, my hair, my body
To see if I had changed much.
I would be nervous and comment on the weather, perhaps,
Attempting to make conversation.

And then you came!
There were many people at the station,
But they might have been buildings or marble statues
For all the attention you paid them
As you hurried forth.
Your crushing embrace, your warm mouth over mine
Blotted them out completely.
And in that one blissful moment
It was as if we had both been lost in strange worlds
And had at last found the way back home.

Obsession Renewed

I thought I cared no more — that time and miles
Had rid the wild obsession from my heart.
I'd quite forgot the challenge in your eyes
That pierces my reserve in one swift dart.
I'd placed my heart so carefully on the shelf,
But knew today I'd only fooled myself.

There Is Only One You

There is only one you, and there will always be
Only one you in this heart for me;
Others may pause as they happen by,
And for the moment attract my eye;
Others may flatter and even intrude
To fascinate me for an interlude,

But I will return in a little while
To the spell of your love — the warmth of your smile,
For there's only one you, and there always will be
Only one you in this world for me.

No Wings Yet

Before you went away, we used to spat
In ancient enmity, like dog and cat,
But during those three years your letters read
That I was perfect; so were you I said.
Now that you're home, how nice to re-discover
Your faulty wife and my imperfect lover.

88

Love Fades?

They say that love grows dull when youth has passed —
That passion cools and dying embers taunt —
That happiness like ours can never last,
And we'll have but the memories to flaunt.

However, when they do unbar the gate
For me to enter into heaven's bliss,
If you should whistle, I would bid them wait
While I returned for one enfeebled kiss.

Home-Coming

I do not understand what brings you here
Who chose the path of freedom yesterday;
There were no bitter words to wound and sear,
Just one brief note and you were on your way.

While night stretched into black eternity,
I lived again each moment we had spent,
Trying to fathom why you went from me,
Some hasty word or action to repent.

I can not understand what brings you here —
Nor let you know how glad I am, my dear.

Winter Hearthspun

Maturity

I tried to make a sculpture
Of the virtues you had shown —
A perfect, shining idol
To be kept upon a throne.

What I had thought was marble
In reality was clay.
And it cracked beneath my chisel
To my heart's complete dismay.

But experience brings wisdom,
With contentment in its girth;
The years have taught this sculptor
The frailties of earth.

To A Doubting Thomas

You, who face your troubles all alone —
It saddens me to know you cannot find
The comfort and the courage I have known
From telling Jesus of my troubled mind.

Oh how I long for wisdom to impart
The truth — that He so patiently awaits
The privilege to console your weary heart,
But only you can open up the gates

Because to all of us God gave free will,
And yet the peace you always seem to seek
Can only come from Him. Oh, friend be still —
If you will only listen He will speak.

Works of Love

If I can sprinkle seeds of joy
On someone's barren plot
And bring to light some cause for hope
That he has long forgot;
If I can lighten someone's load
That seems too great to bear,
Assuring him his fellow man
Is not too rushed to care;
If I can help renew one faith —
Restoring someone's smile,
My life will be enriched to seem
A little more worthwhile.

Prayer

Dear God: I must not permit myself
to waste even one precious moment
of my life in self-pity. Humbly I give
myself to You and ask that You use
my mind and my hands and feet
to do Your work.

That You let my eyes and ears see and hear
only the good concerning my fellow man
and that You use my mouth to spread that good
and also to speak Your counsel and encouragement.

And since love is the magic sunshine
that warms every human heart,
please let my heart be a fountain
from which is continually flowing
Your love and compassion
for humanity.

Winterettes

Winter's daughters all are charming
In the glitter that they wear —
There's December, so disarming,
With the holly in her hair.

She is warm and gay with customs
Seemingly of world renown.
How I love the way she sparkles
When old Santa comes to town.

January, second child —
The one with spangled skirt of ice
Many frown upon as wild
Because of weather she'll entice.

Some seek February's favor,
Whose sculpturing hands hold much surprise.
For though she is of winter's flavor,
There's springtime's promise in her eyes.

The Christmas Belle

December is a Christmas belle
With holly in her hair;
The old and young beneath her spell
You'll find most everywhere.

They love the picture she portrays
In gay poinsettia gown —
Her sparkling, enchanting ways
Of time and world renown.

Humming a lovely Christmas score,
Her step is light and quick
As she goes running to the door
To welcome old Saint Nick.

Communion

No need for fancy phrases
Between us, is there, friend?
To let each other know that we
Will stand by till the end.

No need for company manners
Our feelings to disguise;
We know the way the other feels
By looking in his eyes.

No need for idle chatter
When one of us is blue
To know the other's sympathy
Is with him through and through.

No need for words, or smiles, or tears
To know we understand,
And even when we are apart,
We clasp the other's hand.

Benediction

This quiet hour that you and I have known —
This respite for my weary, worried mind
Will be a candle in dark hours — alone,
And when I wish to close my eyes and find
Contentment, I will take this candle out
And know again release from every doubt.

Santa's Coming!

Leave cookies on the table, Mom,
For Santa comes tonight —
After traveling from the North Pole
Maybe he'll want a bite.

He'll probably be hungry —
Oh, he may be early, too;
Let's jump in bed, huh, Susan?
For he *will* have lots to do.

Gee, I wish that we could wait for him,
But that just couldn't be,
For if he came and found us up —
No toys for you and me!

I just can't go to sleep now —
Hope he brings us a surprise;
Mom, will you please ask the Sandman
To throw sand into my eyes?

Mom

For the tireless efforts that you spent
To keep us wholesome and content;
For your courage when our skies weren't blue,
And the smile so much a part of you;
For your patience with the tedious tasks
And the questions that a small child asks;
For your stories we so loved to hear,
And a million memories we hold dear;
For the love that's never failed a day,
May God bless you, Mom, in every way.

Daddy

D   is for DEVOTION Daddy gave us,
A   for ALWAYS fair in all he'd do;
D   for DISAPPOINTMENTS he would save us,
D   for all our DREAMS he made come true.
Y   is for the YOUTH he spent upon us
And all the YEARS of courage he has shown.
Put them all together, they spell DADDY —
A finer man we've never known!

Cocoa's Christmas

There was silence in the big toy store —
Christmas Eve had brought crowds galore;
But now they had gone, and the lights were low,
And the counters were bare in the afterglow,
But way, way up on the tiptop shelf
Sat Cocoa, the teddy bear, all by himself.

The tears trickled down from his big brown eyes.
He had wanted so very much to surprise
Some little girl or boy tomorrow,
And here he was left by himself in sorrow.
They had picked him up and put him down
Till he felt like the most unloved bear in town.

When suddenly somebody opened wide
The big front door — and who stepped inside?
None other than Santa Claus — on his back
Was the biggest and bulgiest toy-filled sack,
"Come along, little friend," his jolly voice said,
"While little Henry's asleep in bed
I will put you under the Christmas tree,
And tomorrow a proud little boy he'll be."

So away they went in old Santa's sleigh,
And when Henry awoke on Christmas day
To find Cocoa waiting with all his charms
To be taken into his loving arms,
He shouted with glee, "Oh, Mommy, look!
Just like the bear in my story book!"
He kissed him and took him to show his friends —
And so the story of Cocoa ends.

Neighborliness

When you see a neighbor groping
In the path along life's way
For a hand that's warm and steady
And a heart that's light and gay,

Don't pretend you didn't notice
And leave him to his care,
For tomorrow it may be you
In the lonely pathway there.

Clasp his hand and make it hearty;
Let him know your feeling's kind,
And perhaps with just a word you
Can restore his peace of mind.

Tell him that the folk are for him —
Not against him. Unshed tears
Will be transformed into rainbows
When you calm his silent fears.

Love Is A Gift of God

Love is a gift of God. It is far more precious than any material thing one could ever hope to possess. It can't be purchased, for along with all of the best things in life, it is free. Its magic can change a dreary world into a heaven on earth. Its radiance is beyond human power of description. It is not restricted by race, creed or public opinion and has nothing to do with physical appearance, for "beauty is in the eyes of the beholder." There is no fault or shortcoming that love can not overcome with charity and understanding. It does not imprison, but rather, in loving, one is set free. There is no limit to what love can accomplish, for its depth finds qualities that would otherwise remain undiscovered. It is the most beautiful, the most absorbing, and the most rewarding thing in life and by far the most important. For love is truly a gift of God.

Thy Will—Not Mine

Thy will be done, O Father mine —
I put myself into Your hands.
Your love is real — I need no sign
For proof — Your dear heart understands
My frailties — I shed no tear —
Thy will, not mine, O Father dear!

The Master's Plea

To the Worried

Come — come with Me out of the fog of fear —
Roll back the anxious clouds about;
Reminisce only of things held dear;
Forget the events that have caused you doubt.

Come — come with Me into the light of love —
Throw open the windows of your soul;
Let the bright sunshine from above
Illumine the way to your cherished goal.

Unfathomable

I've never met a someone quite like you,
With understanding boundless as the skies;
Another's soul I've never looked into
And found the whole of living in his eyes.

With others I am always reticent;
To you, I bare my innermost desires;
The hours with you seem filled with deep content;
I come away rekindled by strange fires.

What powers have you that set so wholly right
My heart when I am troubled and depressed
And rouse me to a greater strength to fight
My battles with new courage, added zest?

I know you well, yet know you not at all —
Sometimes I think you see through Heaven's wall.

Shrimp Fleet

End of Day

Sometimes I've had the feeling
As I watched the setting sun
That life was swiftly passing by,
And soon it will be done.

As I stood there filled with reverence
For nature's wondrous way
I asked myself the question,
What good have I done today?

To my less fortunate neighbor
Did I lend a helping hand?
Did I listen to his woes and
Really try to understand?

Have I reached a rung that's higher
On the ladder toward my goal?
Have I taken out a moment for
Communion with my soul?

Was I honest with my fellow man
And also with myself?
Did I admit when I was wrong,
Putting pride upon the shelf?

Have I been a friend to those I met
In the things I did and said?
And when tempted to speak sharply
Did I count to ten instead?

Did I take time out to laugh — to love —
To think — to see — to pray?
These are the thoughts that cross my mind
As I watch the dying day.